Rebecca Manley Pippert

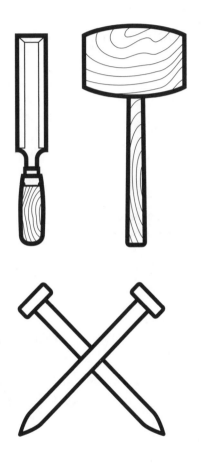

Seven encounters with Jesus
from the Gospel of John

Read Becky's comments on each
of the questions in this guide at:

the**goodbook**.com/discoveringrealguide

Discovering the Real Jesus
© Rebecca Manley Pippert 2016. Reprinted 2018.

This material was previously published as
Looking at the Life of Jesus (Intervarsity Press, 2003)

Published by
The Good Book Company
Tel (US): 866 244 2165
Tel (UK): 0333 123 0880
International: +44 (0) 208 942 0880
Email (US): info@thegoodbook.com
Email (UK): info@thegoodbook.co.uk

the**goodbook**
COMPANY

Websites:
North America: www.thegoodbook.com
UK: www.thegoodbook.co.uk
Australia: www.thegoodbook.com.au
New Zealand: www.thegoodbook.co.nz

Becky Pippert
MINISTRIES

ISBN: 9781784980757 | Printed in Turkey

Design by André Parker

Contents

INTRODUCTION

Discover, investigate, and examine the evidence...

Someone once said that "the unexamined life is not worth living." Yet leading an examined life in our unexamining age is quite a challenge. The pressure and pace of life leave little time for reflection—and people are paying a steep price for it. We are left searching for something worth living for and for some way to be at peace with ourselves, to calm the inner conflicts and feelings of personal inadequacy that make us so dissatisfied with ourselves. How can we discover and live with a deeper sense of life's meaning?

Jesus said, "Come to me, all you who are weary and burdened, and I will give you rest" (Matthew 11 v 28). It is a remarkable statement made by a remarkable man. Jesus insisted that if we desire to find joy, peace and inner transformation, then he's our man. So if his claims are true, if he really is who he says he is, then according to Jesus, to miss him would be to miss life itself.

I vividly remember the first time I read the Gospel of John as an agnostic seeker. My impression of Jesus was that he was sincere and kind, wearing an otherworldly, beatific smile. Then I started reading the Bible. I was not prepared for what I discovered. Here was a man who claimed to be the Messiah, the Prince of Peace, yet he threw furniture down the front steps of the Jerusalem Temple. The religious accused him of being a drunk and a glutton, and having terrible taste in friends. He claimed to be the Son of God; yet one of the chief complaints against him was that he wasn't religious enough! This was not the kind of Jesus I had expected to encounter.

Maybe you're at the same place I was, and you've never read the Bible before. Or perhaps you vaguely remember Bible stories from your childhood but you've never looked at the life of Christ with a discerning, adult mind. Whatever your story, one thing is certain: it's impossible to make an informed decision without first knowing the facts. I wrote this guide for anyone who is genuinely seeking, who has honest questions and who wants to take a fresh look at the real Jesus.

Becky

ABOUT JOHN'S GOSPEL

Since my own journey began in skepticism, where I was encouraged to ask questions and never asked to adopt belief blindly, I have chosen a similar approach in these Bible discussions. It is not necessary that you believe in Jesus or accept the Bible as "divinely inspired" in order to use this guide. Rather, come to the accounts of Jesus as you would to any sound history, with an open mind and heart to see what you find.

This guide is based on the Gospel of John, which most scholars conclude was written by John, one of the twelve disciples of Jesus. When John sat down to write his Gospel, there were already three other Gospels in existence: Matthew, Mark and Luke. The best evidence points to a composition date around AD 90, and he most likely wrote it from Ephesus, which was located in what is modern-day Turkey. Throughout the Gospel, John never mentions himself by name, instead referring to himself simply as "the disciple whom Jesus loved."

John offers a fascinating perspective on the life of Jesus because he was an eyewitness to most of the events he writes about. He followed Jesus from the very beginning of his ministry, and he was one of the inner circle of Jesus' three closest friends. When Jesus was on the cross, it was to John that he entrusted the care of his mother.

The guide includes seven stories from the life of Jesus so that you may begin to get a sense of his person, his teaching, his actions and his claims. John's deepest desire in writing this book was "that you may believe that Jesus is the Messiah, the Son of God" (John 20 v 31). For John was convinced, as I now am, that it is through faith in Jesus that we become fully alive and truly human.

Profits or prophets?

Profits or prophets?

Question

What are common complaints that people have against organized religious institutions such as the church?

Historical context

We are about to read a story of how Jesus responded to the hypocrisy and greed of some of the religious leaders of his day. If you believe that "gentle Jesus meek and mild" is an accurate historical portrayal of Jesus, then you may be in for a surprise.

This is Jesus' first official public appearance in Jerusalem: the religious, political, educational and cultural capital of the Jews. In our age of extreme political correctness, it is astonishing to see Jesus break every possible rule of perceived correctness. The occasion was the great annual celebration of the Passover, when all good Jews made the pilgrimage to the Holy City to observe commemoration of God's mighty historical rescue of his people from Egyptian slavery. The pilgrims came for two primary reasons—(1) to worship God (by making animal sacrifices) and (2) to pray.

When it was almost time for the Jewish Passover, Jesus went up to Jerusalem. [14] In the temple courts he found people selling cattle, sheep and doves, and others sitting at tables exchanging money. [15] So he made a whip out of cords, and drove all from the temple courts, both sheep and cattle; he scattered the coins of the money changers and overturned their tables. [16] To those who sold doves he said, "Get these out of here! Stop turning my Father's house into a market!" [17] His disciples remembered that it is written: "Zeal for your house will consume me."

[18] The Jews then responded to him, "What sign can you show us to prove your authority to do all this?"

[19] Jesus answered them, "Destroy this temple, and I will raise it again in three days."

[20] They replied, "It has taken forty-six years to build this temple, and you are going to raise it in three days?" [21] But the temple he had spoken of was his body. [22] After he was raised from the dead, his disciples recalled what he had said. Then they believed the scripture and the words that Jesus had spoken.

[23] Now while he was in Jerusalem at the Passover Festival, many people saw the signs he was performing and believed in his name. [24] But Jesus would not entrust himself to them, for he knew all people. [25] He did not need any testimony about mankind, for he knew what was in each person.

Note: The small numbers in the Bible passages refer to the numbers of the verses.

1 Imagine the thousands of pilgrims crowding the streets and courtyards of the great temple. What can you hear? See? Smell? What is the mood of the people?

2 What provoked Jesus' anger?

3 What suggests that this wasn't an impulsive act of simply losing his temper (v 15)?

④ There were other people who undoubtedly saw what was happening in the temple precincts. Why was Jesus the only one who was so outraged?

What is significant about how Jesus speaks of God in verse 16?

⑤ Verse 17 is quoting Psalm 69 v 9, which is part of the Jewish Scriptures (and now in the Old Testament part of the Bible). What does this Old Testament verse reveal was motivating Jesus' passionate response?

Picture the scene: a hitherto unknown man walks into the magnificent temple precincts. In the intimidating presence of the priests of the temple, he not only turns tables upside down but directly challenges them, saying, *How dare you turn my Father's house into a market?*

⑥ Jesus was a carpenter from the backwoods town of Nazareth. Why do you think these proud religious leaders did not stop Jesus instantly when he began challenging their authority?

The temple was the center of Jewish religion, representing the very presence of the living God. There was no more powerful symbol of God's presence than the temple—it was the place where his people met with him.

⑦ In verse 19, in response to the temple authorities' demand for credentials, Jesus draws a comparison between himself and the temple. What is he implicitly claiming about himself? Why is this hugely significant?

⑧ In what tone of voice do you suppose verse 20 was spoken?

⑨ The disciples didn't immediately grasp what Jesus was talking about when he said, "Destroy this temple, and I will raise it again in three days." But after Jesus' death and resurrection this incident came to the minds of the disciples and it encouraged them. Why?

⑩ If people were believing in Jesus because of the miraculous signs, why didn't Jesus "entrust himself to them" (v 23-25)?

⑪ Contrast the Pharisees' attitudes and Jesus' attitudes toward God, common people and religious hypocrisy.

Live what you learn

What would you say to a person who is fed up with religious hypocrisy regarding what you have learned about Jesus thus far?

"[I was given the impression] that Jesus was a gentle creature ... [Then] I looked at the New Testament. There I found an account, not in the least of a person with his hair parted in the middle or his hands clasped in appeal, but of an extraordinary being with lips of thunder and acts of lurid decision, flinging down tables, casting out devils, passing with the wild secrecy of the wind. ... The [language] used about Christ has been, perhaps wisely, sweet and submissive. But the [language] used by Christ is quite curiously gigantesque [i.e. big]; it is full of camels leaping through needles and mountains hurled into the sea. ... He flung furniture down the front steps of the Temple and asked men how they expected to escape the damnation of Hell."

G. K. CHESTERTON, *ORTHODOXY*

G. K. Chesterton (1874-1936) was a journalist, an essayist, a humorist and one of the most brilliant defenders of the Christian faith in the twentieth century. In an age of pessimism and doubt he powerfully defended the faith in debates with such renowned figures as George Bernard Shaw. A prolific author, his most famous books are *Orthodoxy* and the Father Brown detective stories. Here we read his surprise at having first encountered the Jesus described in the Bible.

Notes

15

2

Water for a dry soul

JOHN 4 v 5-42

Water for a dry soul

What common social boundaries exist in our culture that most of us would be unlikely to cross?

Historical context

We are about to read a story in which Jesus does the inconceivable. In his culture it was considered the height of impropriety for a religious man to talk with a woman; but to speak to a woman of low moral standing was unheard of. Consider these rabbinic warnings taught by the Jewish leaders of Jesus' day: "One should not talk with a woman on the street, not even with his own wife, and certainly not with someone else's wife, because of the gossip of men." "It is forbidden to give a woman any greeting."

Besides ignoring these social prejudices, Jesus overlooked the deep racial and religious prejudice that Jews felt toward Samaritans. The feelings of antagonism were mutual; the Samaritans often refused lodging to Jews passing though their territory, so Jews often traveled to the east side of the Jordan River to avoid Samaria. The bitterness between Jews and Samaritans was at its height in Jesus' day.

Now [Jesus] had to go through Samaria. ⁵ So he came to a town in Samaria called Sychar, near the plot of ground Jacob had given to his son Joseph. ⁶ Jacob's well was there, and Jesus, tired as he was from the journey, sat down by the well. It was about noon.

⁷ When a Samaritan woman came to draw water, Jesus said to her, "Will you give me a drink?" ⁸ (His disciples had gone into the town to buy food.)

⁹ The Samaritan woman said to him, "You are a Jew and I am a Samaritan woman. How can you ask me for a drink?" (For Jews do not associate with Samaritans.)

¹⁰ Jesus answered her, "If you knew the gift of God and who it is that asks you for a drink, you would have asked him and he would have given you living water."

¹¹ "Sir," the woman said, "you have nothing to draw with and the well is deep. Where can you get this living water? ¹² Are you greater than our father Jacob, who gave us the well and drank from it himself, as did also his sons and his livestock?"

¹³ Jesus answered, "Everyone who drinks this water will be thirsty again, ¹⁴ but whoever drinks the water I give them will never thirst. Indeed, the water I give them will become in them a spring of water welling up to eternal life."

¹⁵ The woman said to him, "Sir, give me this water so that I won't get thirsty and have to keep coming here to draw water."

1 Why have Jesus and his disciples stopped at Sychar?

List everything you can about Jesus' physical and mental state (v 6-8).

2 Consider the hot Middle-Eastern climate. Why do you think the woman is drawing water at midday?

3 Why is the woman initially shocked at Jesus' request? List all the cultural barriers crossed already.

4 We will soon discover that in the morally conservative, traditional culture of Jesus' day this woman has a troubled history with men. Yet Jesus begins his conversation with her by sharing his personal need, rather than first addressing her problem. What does this reveal about Jesus' understanding of human nature and his sensitivity to this woman in particular?

5 How would you describe the woman's reaction to Jesus' offer in verses 11-12? Do you think she understands?

6 What does Jesus say about this "living water" that makes it so appealing to her (v 13-14)?

Later, in John 7 v 37-39, Jesus offers eternal life through the gift of the Holy Spirit to all who believe in him—this is what he means by this "living water". "Let anyone who is thirsty come to me and drink. Whoever believes in me, as Scripture has said, rivers of living water will flow from within them."

READ SOURCE TEXT: JOHN 4 v 16-30

He told her, "Go, call your husband and come back."
¹⁷ "I have no husband," she replied.

Jesus said to her, "You are right when you say you have no husband. ¹⁸ The fact is, you have had five husbands, and the man you now have is not your husband. What you have just said is quite true."

¹⁹ "Sir," the woman said, "I can see that you are a prophet. ²⁰ Our ancestors worshiped on this mountain, but you Jews claim that the place where we must worship is in Jerusalem."

²¹ "Woman," Jesus replied, "believe me, a time is coming when you will worship the Father neither on this mountain nor in Jerusalem. ²² You Samaritans worship what you do not know; we worship what we do know, for salvation is from the Jews. ²³ Yet a time is coming and has now come when the true worshipers will worship the Father in the Spirit and in truth, for they are the kind of worshipers the Father seeks. ²⁴ God is spirit, and his worshipers must worship in the Spirit and in truth."

²⁵ The woman said, "I know that Messiah" (called Christ) "is

coming. When he comes, he will explain everything to us."

²⁶ Then Jesus declared, "I, the one speaking to you—I am he."

²⁷ Just then his disciples returned and were surprised to find him talking with a woman. But no one asked, "What do you want?" or "Why are you talking with her?"

²⁸ Then, leaving her water jar, the woman went back to the town and said to the people, ²⁹ "Come, see a man who told me everything I ever did. Could this be the Messiah?" ³⁰ They came out of the town and made their way toward him.

7 This is a crucial point in the conversation. Just when the woman asks to receive this living water, Jesus suddenly delves into her personal life and asks her to go call her husband. Why?

8 Jesus affirms her for answering honestly, but why do you think he brings up her list of past marriages and present problematic relationship (v 17-18)?

9 No doubt stunned by Jesus' knowledge of her personal life, she changes the subject to the controversy over the proper place of worship (v 19-20). What does Jesus teach about true worship (v 22- 24)?

Both Jews and Samaritans were awaiting the arrival of the Messiah—the chosen king God had promised, who would rescue people from sin. During her conversation with Jesus, this woman is beginning to wonder if this man might possibly be the Messiah they'd been waiting for.

10 Note the disciples' reaction upon returning to the scene. How do you think the woman felt, knowing that Jesus didn't ignore her when they arrived (v 27)?

READ SOURCE TEXT: JOHN 4 v 39-42

Many of the Samaritans from that town believed in him because of the woman's testimony, "He told me everything I've ever done." ⁴⁰ So when the Samaritans came to him, they urged him to stay with them, and he stayed two days. ⁴¹ And because of his words many more became believers.

⁴² They said to the woman, "We no longer believe just because of what you said; now we have heard for ourselves, and we know that this man really is the Savior of the world."

11 Describe the woman's message to the townspeople and their response (v 39-42).

12 What was it about her encounter with Jesus that freed her to be so transparent about her life?

Live what you learn

The religious and respectable people of Jesus' day would have regarded this woman as a lost cause. Even his own disciples were shocked that Jesus was speaking to her. What did Jesus see in her and her predicament (her "thirst") that apparently no one else did?

How does it affect your attitude to others, or even to yourself, to know that Jesus considers no one a lost cause?

"I may, I suppose, regard myself, or pass for being, a relatively successful man. People occasionally stare at me in the streets—that's fame. I can fairly easily earn enough to qualify for admission to the higher slopes of the Inland Revenue [the equivalent of the Internal Revenue Service]—that's success. Furnished with money and a little of success even the elderly, if they care to, may partake of trendy diversions—that's pleasure. It might happen once in a while that something I said or wrote was sufficiently heeded for me to persuade myself that it represented a significant impact on our time—that's fulfillment. Yet I say to you—and I beg you to believe me—multiply these tiny triumphs by a million, add them all together, and they are nothing—less than nothing, a positive impediment— measured against one draught of that living water Christ offers to the spiritually thirsty, irrespective of who or what they are."

MALCOLM MUGGERIDGE, AS CITED IN J. GLADSTONE, *LIVING WITH STYLE*

Malcolm Muggeridge (1903-1990), an English journalist and former editor of *Punch* magazine, was known for his great satiric wit and devastating political and social critiques. A celebrated and outspoken skeptic of the Christian faith, his conversion to Christianity in his mid-life was an astonishment to his public and to himself! Read about his faith journey in *Chronicles of Wasted Years* or the Christian thinkers who most inspired him in his book *A Third Testament*. It was Muggeridge who is credited for introducing Mother Teresa to the world stage in his book *Something Beautiful for God*.

Notes

3

Soul food

Soul food

Question

Sooner or later most of us face an impossible situation that leaves us feeling inadequate. Do you think seeing our inadequacies is helpful or harmful? What types of things do people often turn to for help?

Historical context

In the passage we are reading today, Jesus' disciples come up against the reality of their own inadequacies in seemingly impossible situations.

This event takes place around the end of Jesus' second year of ministry. A year has passed since Jesus turned the tables over in the Jerusalem Temple (John 2). During this time Jesus has ministered largely in and around Galilee.

In Mark 6 v 30-31 we learn that the disciples have just returned from a highly successful preaching tour and they need rest. To get privacy Jesus takes his disciples to the hills to the east of the Sea of Galilee, also known as the Golan Heights. But the crowd, who has heard of Jesus' miracles among the sick, gets wind of Jesus' whereabouts and follows him round the lake.

Some time after this, Jesus crossed to the far shore of the Sea of Galilee (that is, the Sea of Tiberias), ² and a great crowd of people followed him because they saw the signs he had performed by healing those who were ill. ³ Then Jesus went up on a mountainside and sat down with his disciples. ⁴ The Jewish Passover Festival was near.

⁵ When Jesus looked up and saw a great crowd coming toward him, he said to Philip, "Where shall we buy bread for these people to eat?" ⁶ He asked this only to test him, for he already had in mind what he was going to do.

⁷ Philip answered him, "It would take more than half a year's wages to buy enough bread for each one to have a bite!"

⁸ Another of his disciples, Andrew, Simon Peter's brother, spoke up, ⁹ "Here is a boy with five small barley loaves and two small fish, but how far will they go among so many?"

¹⁰ Jesus said, "Have the people sit down." There was plenty of grass in that place, and they sat down (about five thousand men were there). ¹¹ Jesus then took the loaves, gave thanks, and distributed to those who were seated as much as they wanted. He did the same with the fish.

¹² When they had all had enough to eat, he said to his disciples, "Gather the pieces that are left over. Let nothing be wasted." ¹³ So they gathered them and filled twelve baskets with the pieces of the five barley loaves left over by those who had eaten.

¹⁴ After the people saw the sign Jesus performed, they began to say, "Surely this is the Prophet who is to come into the world." ¹⁵ Jesus, knowing that they intended to come and make him king by force, withdrew again to a mountain by himself.

From the information in verses 2-5, describe the situation. (Why have the crowd followed Jesus? What is Jesus doing? What are the people doing?)

2 If Jesus knew what he was going to do (v 6), why did he ask his disciples how they could feed the crowd?

3 How did Philip, who was from nearby Bethsaida and thus knew the territory well, respond to Jesus' question (v 5-7)?

4 Why do you think Jesus was unperturbed by the offering of such a measly resource for such a vast crowd (v 9)?

5 How do you think the disciples and the people sitting on the grass might have felt as they heard Jesus giving thanks for the food (v 10-11)?

6 How do you think the disciples felt as they collected up the pieces left over (v 12-13)?

7 In Moses' day, God supernaturally fed his people manna, a bread that came from heaven. Therefore, the crowd concludes this is the prophet whom Moses had said would come. What was Jesus' response to the people saying that he would become a political king (v 14-15)?

8 In both verses 3 and 15 we see Jesus withdraw from the people. Why do you think he does this?

READ SOURCE TEXT: JOHN 6 v 25-35

When they found him on the other side of the lake, they asked him, "Rabbi, when did you get here?"

²⁶ Jesus answered, "Very truly I tell you, you are looking for me, not because you saw the signs I performed but because you ate the loaves and had your fill. ²⁷ Do not work for food that spoils, but for food that endures to eternal life, which the Son of Man will give you. For on him God the Father has placed his seal of approval."

²⁸ Then they asked him, "What must we do to do the works God requires?"

²⁹ Jesus answered, "The work of God is this: to believe in the one he has sent."

³⁰ So they asked him, "What sign then will you give that we may

see it and believe you? What will you do? [31] Our ancestors ate the manna in the wilderness; as it is written: 'He gave them bread from heaven to eat.'"

[32] Jesus said to them, "Very truly I tell you, it is not Moses who has given you the bread from heaven, but it is my Father who gives you the true bread from heaven. [33] For the bread of God is the bread that comes down from heaven and gives life to the world."

[34] "Sir," they said, "always give us this bread."

[35] Then Jesus declared, "I am the bread of life. Whoever comes to me will never go hungry, and whoever believes in me will never be thirsty."

9 How does Jesus assess the crowd's motive in searching for him, and what is their main error (v 25-27)?

10 As long as people came to Jesus seeking only physical things (free food and a political Messiah who would rid them of Roman rule), Jesus knew their deepest needs would go unmet. What does Jesus want them to focus on (v 27, 29)?

11 What do you think Jesus meant when he called himself the bread of life? How will this satisfy their deepest needs (v 35)?

Live what you learn

The crowd was so obsessed with getting their physical needs met that they failed to understand Jesus' greater offer to meet their deepest needs and yearnings. How can our immediate needs or worries blind us from seeing our deeper spiritual needs?

How can our problems bring us closer to God instead?

"You promised them the Bread of Heaven, but I repeat again, can it compare with earthly bread in the eyes of the weak, ever sinful and ever ignoble race? ... Yet in this question lies hidden the great secret of this world. Choosing [Christ's] 'bread,' you would have satisfied the universal and everlasting craving of humanity—to find someone to worship. So long as man remains free he strives for nothing so incessantly and so painfully as to find someone to worship. ... For the secret of man's being is not only to live but to have something to live for. Without a clear conception of the object of life, man would not consent to go on living and would rather destroy himself than remain on earth, though he had bread in abundance."

FYODOR DOSTOYEVSKY, *THE BROTHERS KARAMAZOV*

Dostoyevsky (1821-1881) was a Russian novelist whose brilliance was matched by a life full of contradictions and paradoxes. He was frequently in debt, subject to epileptic seizures, and plagued by tragedy and loss. Yet he slowly came to the conclusion that only faith in God could make life meaningful and lift humankind from its tragic and fallen condition. This excerpt is from the legendary chapter "The Grand Inquisitor" in *The Brothers Karamazov*. Ivan, an intellectual atheist, rigorously defends his doubts and rejection of God to his novice monk brother, Alyosha, through a prose poem he has written in which the Grand Inquisitor ridicules the Divine Visitor. Ironically, his very attack against Christ still provides arguments for faith.

Notes

4

I once was
blind...

I once was blind...

Question

What fears do you have about what others might think if they discover you are reading the Bible and have spiritual questions?

Historical context

We are about to read a passage in which a genuine spiritual seeker comes to believe in Jesus and then experiences repercussions and even persecution for his faith. This story is about a man who gets caught in the political meat grinder of religious politics. He reminds us of how important it is to stay open to the truth and to not allow any preconceived views or agendas to keep us from experiencing God's truth.

The Jewish rabbis of Jesus' day believed that people suffered disabilities because of their sin or the sin of their parents. Eastern religion also teaches that our sins in this life will come and haunt us in the next life. Jesus defies the notion that our "karma" or our present suffering can always be blamed on our sin or that of others. Instead, Jesus teaches and performs a miracle that sets a man free from decades of shame and suffering.

As [Jesus] went along, he saw a man blind from birth. ² His disciples asked him, "Rabbi, who sinned, this man or his parents, that he was born blind?"

³ "Neither this man nor his parents sinned," said Jesus, "but this happened so that the works of God might be displayed in him. ⁴ As long as it is day, we must do the works of him who sent me. Night is coming, when no one can work. ⁵ While I am in the world, I am the light of the world."

Based on the question the disciples ask Jesus (v 2), what do they believe was the cause of this man's suffering?

❷ How does Jesus' response to the disciples' question give suffering people hope (v 3)?

After saying this, he spit on the ground, made some mud with the saliva, and put it on the man's eyes. ⁷ "Go," he told him, "wash in the Pool of Siloam" (this word means "Sent"). So the man went and washed, and came home seeing.

⁸ His neighbors and those who had formerly seen him begging asked, "Isn't this the same man who used to sit and beg?" ⁹ Some claimed that he was.

Others said, "No, he only looks like him."

But he himself insisted, "I am the man."

¹⁰ "How then were your eyes opened?" they asked.

¹¹ He replied, "The man they call Jesus made some mud and put it on my eyes. He told me to go to Siloam and wash. So I went and

washed, and then I could see."

¹² "Where is this man?" they asked him.

"I don't know," he said.

¹³ They brought to the Pharisees the man who had been blind.

 Imagine you are the blind beggar. We are told that a blind person has exquisite senses in other areas. What would he have heard, felt or sensed from Jesus' interaction with him, do you think?

4 Jesus healed people in widely different ways. Why do you think Jesus goes through the process of making mud and instructs the man to go wash, instead of healing him instantly?

~~Describe what it would have been like for the healed man to see vivid colors and people's expressions for the first time.~~

How did the people who knew him respond (v 8-13)?

6 How does Jesus' miracle confirm his earlier spiritual claim in verse 5?

READ SOURCE TEXT: JOHN 9 v 14-34

Now the day on which Jesus had made the mud and opened the man's eyes was a Sabbath. ¹⁵ Therefore the Pharisees also asked him how he had received his sight. "He put mud on my eyes," the man replied, "and I washed, and now I see."

¹⁶ Some of the Pharisees said, "This man is not from God, for he does not keep the Sabbath."

But others asked, "How can a sinner perform such signs?" So they were divided.

¹⁷ Then they turned again to the blind man, "What have you to say about him? It was your eyes he opened."

The man replied, "He is a prophet."

¹⁸ They still did not believe that he had been blind and had received his sight until they sent for the man's parents. ¹⁹ "Is this your son?" they asked. "Is this the one you say was born blind? How is it that now he can see?"

²⁰ "We know he is our son," the parents answered, "and we know

he was born blind. ²¹ But how he can see now, or who opened his eyes, we don't know. Ask him. He is of age; he will speak for himself." ²² His parents said this because they were afraid of the Jewish leaders, who already had decided that anyone who acknowledged that Jesus was the Messiah would be put out of the synagogue. ²³ That was why his parents said, "He is of age; ask him."

²⁴ A second time they summoned the man who had been blind. "Give glory to God by telling the truth," they said. "We know this man is a sinner."

²⁵ He replied, "Whether he is a sinner or not, I don't know. One thing I do know. I was blind but now I see!"

²⁶ Then they asked him, "What did he do to you? How did he open your eyes?"

²⁷ He answered, "I have told you already and you did not listen. Why do you want to hear it again? Do you want to become his disciples too?"

²⁸ Then they hurled insults at him and said, "You are this fellow's disciple! We are disciples of Moses! ²⁹ We know that God spoke to Moses, but as for this fellow, we don't even know where he comes from."

³⁰ The man answered, "Now that is remarkable! You don't know where he comes from, yet he opened my eyes. ³¹ We know that God does not listen to sinners. He listens to the godly person who does his will. ³² Nobody has ever heard of opening the eyes of a man born blind. ³³ If this man were not from God, he could do nothing."

³⁴ To this they replied, "You were steeped in sin at birth; how dare you lecture us!" And they threw him out.

7 Why do some of the Pharisees object to this miracle (v 16, 22, 24, 29)?

In the Bible, God created the Sabbath for his people's good; so they could rest from their daily work and devote time to worshiping God. But the Pharisees had exaggerated God's commands with countless extra laws that were a burden to keep. When Jesus healed on the Sabbath, he demonstrated the true application of God's laws—that "it is lawful to do good on the Sabbath" (Matthew 12 v 12). The "law" that Jesus violated was a man-made rule that was itself against the principles of God's law.

8 Still skeptical, the Pharisees send for the man's parents. Why were the blind man's parents so cautious as they answered their questions (v 18-23)?

9 Trace this unnamed man's understanding of Jesus' identity so far: look at verses 11, 17, 31 and 33.

What strikes you about how he now answers the Pharisees' unreasonable objections (v 30-33)?

10 How do the Pharisees react when they are at a loss to prove the miracle didn't occur (v 28-34)?

READ SOURCE TEXT: JOHN 9 v 35-41

Jesus heard that they had thrown him out, and when he found him, he said, "Do you believe in the Son of Man?"

36 "Who is he, sir?" the man asked. "Tell me so that I may believe in him."

37 Jesus said, "You have now seen him; in fact, he is the one speaking with you."

38 Then the man said, "Lord, I believe," and he worshiped him.

39 Jesus said, "For judgment I have come into this world, so that the blind will see and those who see will become blind."

40 Some Pharisees who were with him heard him say this and asked, "What? Are we blind too?"

41 Jesus said, "If you were blind, you would not be guilty of sin; but now that you claim you can see, your guilt remains."

11 For what two reasons did Jesus seek out the healed man the second time?

12 The man worships Jesus in verse 38. How would you describe the range of emotions this man has experienced throughout the events of this story?

13 What kept the religious leaders from seeing the truth?

Live what you learn

We learn from this man's story that faith is a process. How have your ideas about God changed over the years and why?

The shame and suffering of this man's life was clearly alleviated by Jesus' healing. Yet there were serious repercussions for him in coming to believe in Jesus. How can a full commitment to faith in Christ cause tensions in a person's life even today?

"Amazing grace! how sweet the sound
that saved a wretch like me!
I once was lost but now am found,
Was blind, but now I see.
'Twas grace that taught my heart to fear,
And grace my fears relieved,
How precious did that grace appear
The hour I first believed."

JOHN NEWTON, "AMAZING GRACE"

John Newton (1725-1807), the author of this beloved hymn, was a British sailor whose life of debauchery and sin took him to the western coast of Africa, where he eventually got involved in the African slave trade. His dramatic conversion during a violent storm in the North Atlantic changed his life forever. He sought orders to become an Anglican clergyman, served as spiritual counselor to influential leaders and wrote hundreds of hymns, including "Amazing Grace." In his later years he played a leading role in Wilberforce's political campaign against slave trading.

Sarah → 1st question
Evy → context

passage 1 + q 2

passage 2 + q 4/6

passage 3 + q 7/9/10, Sarah speak
after →

passage 4 + q 11/13

Evy → 1st end ?
Sarah → second end ?

Evy → goals
Sarah → pray

5

Dead man
walking

JOHN 11 v 1-44

Dead man walking

Question

What are some of your honest feelings and fears about death—especially when a family member or a friend dies?

Historical context

We are about to read a story in which a beloved friend of Jesus dies. You may be surprised, even shocked, by Jesus' reactions, but it gives us an opportunity to learn more about what Jesus was like and what he thought about death.

When Jesus was last in Jerusalem, the controversy and attacks against him were increasingly intense. The Jews were divided: some believed in him, some said he was demon-possessed, others dismissed him as a lunatic, and still others wondered how an evil man could be used by God to perform miracles. However, at the Festival of Dedication things reached a fever-pitch when Jesus claimed equality with God (10 v 30), which prompted his antagonists to pick up stones to kill him (stoning was the accepted punishment for blasphemy; see John 10 v 33). It was dangerous for Jesus to stay in Jerusalem, and since he knew it wasn't yet his time to die, he left temporarily and began ministering across the Jordan river.

However, while he was there, he received an urgent request for help. His dear friend Lazarus, the brother of Mary and Martha, was very sick. These friends lived in Bethany, a few miles southeast from Jerusalem, where Jesus had been a frequent guest in their home. Lazarus and his sisters felt great affection for Jesus and he for them.

49

Now a man named Lazarus was sick. He was from Bethany, the village of Mary and her sister Martha. ² (This Mary, whose brother Lazarus now lay sick, was the same one who poured perfume on the Lord and wiped his feet with her hair.) ³ So the sisters sent word to Jesus, "Lord, the one you love is sick."

⁴ When he heard this, Jesus said, "This sickness will not end in death. No, it is for God's glory so that God's Son may be glorified through it." ⁵ Now Jesus loved Martha and her sister and Lazarus. ⁶ So when he heard that Lazarus was sick, he stayed where he was two more days, ⁷ and then he said to his disciples, "Let us go back to Judea."

⁸ "But Rabbi," they said, "a short while ago the Jews there tried to stone you, and yet you are going back?"

⁹ Jesus answered, "Are there not twelve hours of daylight? Anyone who walks in the daytime will not stumble, for they see by this world's light. ¹⁰ It is when a person walks at night that they stumble, for they have no light."

¹¹ After he had said this, he went on to tell them, "Our friend Lazarus has fallen asleep; but I am going there to wake him up."

¹² His disciples replied, "Lord, if he sleeps, he will get better." ¹³ Jesus had been speaking of his death, but his disciples thought he meant natural sleep.

¹⁴ So then he told them plainly, "Lazarus is dead, ¹⁵ and for your sake I am glad I was not there, so that you may believe. But let us go to him."

¹⁶ Then Thomas (also known as Didymus) said to the rest of the disciples, "Let us also go, that we may die with him."

1 What was Jesus' immediate response when he heard the news about Lazarus (v 4-6)?

2 The text makes it clear that Jesus loves Lazarus; yet he deliberately delays in coming. Jesus would have wanted to go immediately, but what did he know that enabled him to wait (v 4, 15)?

Why was it important that Lazarus' death be firmly established if Jesus' goal was to be accomplished?

3 Why were the disciples shocked at Jesus' decision to go to Judea (v 8)?

4 What reason did Jesus give for going (v 9-15)?

5 How would you characterize Thomas's response (v 16)?

READ SOURCE TEXT: JOHN 11 v 17-27

On his arrival, Jesus found that Lazarus had already been in the tomb for four days. [18] Now Bethany was less than two miles from Jerusalem, [19] and many Jews had come to Martha and Mary to comfort them in the loss of their brother. [20] When Martha heard that Jesus was coming, she went out to meet him, but Mary stayed at home.

[21] "Lord," Martha said to Jesus, "if you had been here, my brother would not have died. [22] But I know that even now God will give you whatever you ask."

[23] Jesus said to her, "Your brother will rise again."

[24] Martha answered, "I know he will rise again in the resurrection at the last day."

[25] Jesus said to her, "I am the resurrection and the life. The one who believes in me will live, even though they die; [26] and whoever lives by believing in me will never die. Do you believe this?"

[27] "Yes, Lord," she replied, "I believe that you are the Messiah, the Son of God, who is to come into the world."

6 Describe the scene as Jesus approached the home of Martha and Mary (v 17-19).

7 What elements of doubt and faith do you see in Martha's response to Jesus (v 20-22, 24, 27)?

8 In verse 24 Martha makes the statement, "I know he will rise again in the resurrection at the last day." But what extraordinary claim does Jesus make that takes her faith even further (v 25-26)?

READ SOURCE TEXT: JOHN 11 v 28-44

After she had said this, she went back and called her sister Mary aside. "The Teacher is here," she said, "and is asking for you." ²⁹ When Mary heard this, she got up quickly and went to him. ³⁰ Now Jesus had not yet entered the village, but was still at the place where Martha had met him. ³¹ When the Jews who had been with Mary in the house, comforting her, noticed how quickly she got up and went out, they followed her, supposing she was going to the tomb to mourn there.

³² When Mary reached the place where Jesus was and saw him, she fell at his feet and said, "Lord, if you had been here, my brother would not have died."

³³ When Jesus saw her weeping, and the Jews who had come along with her also weeping, he was deeply moved in spirit and troubled. ³⁴ "Where have you laid him?" he asked.

"Come and see, Lord," they replied.

³⁵ Jesus wept.

³⁶ Then the Jews said, "See how he loved him!"

³⁷ But some of them said, "Could not he who opened the eyes of the blind man have kept this man from dying?"

³⁸ Jesus, once more deeply moved, came to the tomb. It was a cave with a stone laid across the entrance. ³⁹ "Take away the stone," he said.

"But, Lord," said Martha, the sister of the dead man, "by this time there is a bad odor, for he has been there four days."

⁴⁰ Then Jesus said, "Did I not tell you that if you believe, you will see the glory of God?"

⁴¹ So they took away the stone. Then Jesus looked up and said, "Father, I thank you that you have heard me. ⁴² I knew that you always hear me, but I said this for the benefit of the people standing here, that they may believe that you sent me."

⁴³ When he had said this, Jesus called in a loud voice, "Lazarus, come out!" ⁴⁴ The dead man came out, his hands and feet wrapped with strips of linen, and a cloth around his face.

Jesus said to them, "Take off the grave clothes and let him go."

9 How does John carefully describe the various stages of Jesus' response to the grief and anguish of Mary and those who came with her (v 33, 35, 38)?

10 The words John uses to describe Jesus' response in verse 38, "deeply moved," imply not simply intense grief but deep anger—like a snorting horse on its hind legs. Why do you think Jesus responds to Lazarus' death, and the enormous grief it caused Mary and Martha, not only with compassionate grief but also with outrage?

11 What does Jesus say, through his words and prayer, about the purpose of this event (v 40, 42)?

12 Describe the extraordinary event that took place at Jesus' command. What would it have been like to witness the events of verses 43-44?

Live what you learn

What does this story teach us about our frustration when God seems to delay in answering our prayers?

The natural human yearning is that we and those we love should never die. Do the miracle of Lazarus, and Jesus' words to Martha—"Whoever lives by believing in me will never die" (v 26)—give you hope? Why or why not?

"Creatures are not born with desires unless satisfaction for those desires exists. A baby feels hunger: well, there is such a thing as food. A duckling wants to swim: well, there is such a thing as water ... If I find in myself a desire which no experience in this world can satisfy, the most probable explanation is that I was made for another world ... I must keep alive in myself the desire for my true country, which I shall not find till after death; I must never let it get snowed under or turned aside; I must make it the main object of life to press on to that country and to help others to do the same."

C. S. LEWIS, *MERE CHRISTIANITY*

C. S. Lewis (1898-1963) was a scholar and writer who taught English literature at Oxford and Cambridge Universities in England. Well into his adult life he was a staunch atheist. After his astonishing conversion to Christianity (documented in his book *Surprised by Joy*), he eventually went on to become one of the bestselling Christian authors of all time. For a brilliant and lucid explanation of the Christian faith read *Mere Christianity*; for a look at the nature of evil read *The Screwtape Letters*.

Notes

6

Death isn't the last word

JOHN 19 v 1-37

Death isn't the last word

Question

Every philosophy, every religion and every interpretation of history must explain why the world and human beings are both beautiful and yet so broken. What evidence do you see that human beings need transformation from the inside?

Historical context

Christianity begins with the assumption that human beings are in trouble and need rescuing, and that God has taken the initiative in sending Jesus Christ to deliver them from their dilemma. What follows is the unfolding of God's rescue mission.

The night before the events of this passage, the Roman guards (with the aid of Judas, one of the disciples) arrested Jesus in the Garden of Gethsemane. Next they took Jesus to Annas, a former high priest, who questioned Jesus in an attempt to get evidence to convict him of blasphemy. Then Jesus was sent to the home of Caiaphas, the serving high priest, with Peter and, most likely, John observing from a distance. During the night the Jewish council determined that Jesus should die for blasphemy (Luke 22 v 63-71), but before the Roman authorities they would falsely charge Jesus with treason in order to obtain the death penalty. (Under Roman rule the Jews had no authority to carry out a death penalty.) Upon completing their mock trial in the very early morning, the Jewish leaders took Jesus to the palace of the Roman governor, Pilate.

Pilate interrogates Jesus and finds him innocent. But the Jewish leaders insist that Jesus be crucified. Next follows a series of compromises on Pilate's part, finally leading to his acquiescence to their wishes.

READ SOURCE TEXT: JOHN 19 v 1-16

Then Pilate took Jesus and had him flogged. [2] The soldiers twisted together a crown of thorns and put it on his head. They clothed him in a purple robe [3] and went up to him again and again, saying, "Hail, king of the Jews!" And they slapped him in the face.

[4] Once more Pilate came out and said to the Jews gathered there, "Look, I am bringing him out to you to let you know that I find no basis for a charge against him." [5] When Jesus came out wearing the crown of thorns and the purple robe, Pilate said to them, "Here is the man!"

[6] As soon as the chief priests and their officials saw him, they shouted, "Crucify! Crucify!"

But Pilate answered, "You take him and crucify him. As for me, I find no basis for a charge against him."

[7] The Jewish leaders insisted, "We have a law, and according to that law he must die, because he claimed to be the Son of God."

[8] When Pilate heard this, he was even more afraid, [9] and he went back inside the palace. "Where do you come from?" he asked Jesus, but Jesus gave him no answer. [10] "Do you refuse to speak to me?" Pilate said. "Don't you realize I have power either to free you or to crucify you?"

[11] Jesus answered, "You would have no power over me if it were not given to you from above. Therefore the one who handed me over to you is guilty of a greater sin."

[12] From then on, Pilate tried to set Jesus free, but the Jewish leaders kept shouting, "If you let this man go, you are no friend of Caesar. Anyone who claims to be a king opposes Caesar."

[13] When Pilate heard this, he brought Jesus out and sat down on the judge's seat at a place known as the Stone Pavement (which

in Aramaic is Gabbatha). ¹⁴ It was the day of Preparation of the Passover; it was about noon.

"Here is your king," Pilate said to the Jews.

¹⁵ But they shouted, "Take him away! Take him away! Crucify him!"

"Shall I crucify your king?" Pilate asked.

"We have no king but Caesar," the chief priests answered. ¹⁶ Finally Pilate handed him over to them to be crucified.

So the soldiers took charge of Jesus.

1 What do verses 4, 6 and 12 reveal about Pilate's opinion of Jesus?

2 Flogging practices in those days were brutal as the victim would receive up to forty lashes with a three-pronged metal-tipped rope, usually on the bare backs of those found guilty. Given Pilate's opinion of Jesus, why does Pilate have Jesus flogged, do you think?

3 When the real basis of the Jews' accusation against Jesus is laid bare, how does it increase Pilate's fear (v 7-8)?

4 What is Pilate really asking in verse 9, and why does Jesus not answer?

5 How does Jesus respond to Pilate's claim that he is under Pilate's power (v 10-11)?

6 Despite Pilate's firm intention to set Jesus free, what trap did the Jewish leaders use to coerce him to pronounce the death penalty on a man he knew was innocent (v 12-15)?

READ SOURCE TEXT: JOHN 19 v 17-27

Carrying his own cross, he went out to the place of the Skull (which in Aramaic is called Golgotha). ¹⁸ There they crucified him, and with him two others—one on each side and Jesus in the middle.

¹⁹ Pilate had a notice prepared and fastened to the cross. It read: JESUS OF NAZARETH, THE KING OF THE JEWS. ²⁰ Many of the Jews read this sign, for the place where Jesus was crucified was near the city,

and the sign was written in Aramaic, Latin and Greek. ²¹ The chief priests of the Jews protested to Pilate, "Do not write 'The King of the Jews,' but that this man claimed to be king of the Jews."

²² Pilate answered, "What I have written, I have written."

²³ When the soldiers crucified Jesus, they took his clothes, dividing them into four shares, one for each of them, with the undergarment remaining. This garment was seamless, woven in one piece from top to bottom.

²⁴ "Let's not tear it," they said to one another. "Let's decide by lot who will get it."

This happened that the scripture might be fulfilled that said,

"They divided my clothes among them
    and cast lots for my garment."

So this is what the soldiers did.

²⁵ Near the cross of Jesus stood his mother, his mother's sister, Mary the wife of Clopas, and Mary Magdalene. ²⁶ When Jesus saw his mother there, and the disciple whom he loved standing nearby, he said to her, "Woman, here is your son," ²⁷ and to the disciple, "Here is your mother." From that time on, this disciple took her into his home.

7 Think back on the events of Jesus' last twenty-four hours and describe his physical condition when he is carrying his cross.

8 Why did the Jews object to Pilate's title above Jesus' cross (v 19-21)?

9 How was the Old Testament prophecy of Psalm 22 v 18, quoted in verse 24, fulfilled at the cross (v 23-24)?

10 What wonderful provision does Jesus make for his mother before he dies (v 26-27)?

READ SOURCE TEXT: JOHN 19 v 28-37

Later, knowing that everything had now been finished, and so that Scripture would be fulfilled, Jesus said, "I am thirsty." ²⁹ A jar of wine vinegar was there, so they soaked a sponge in it, put the sponge on a stalk of the hyssop plant, and lifted it to Jesus' lips. [30] When he had received the drink, Jesus said, "It is finished." With that, he bowed his head and gave up his spirit.

[31] Now it was the day of Preparation, and the next day was to be a special Sabbath. Because the Jewish leaders did not want the bodies left on the crosses during the Sabbath, they asked Pilate to have the legs broken and the bodies taken down. [32] The soldiers therefore came and broke the legs of the first man who had been crucified with Jesus, and then those of the other. [33] But when they came to Jesus and found that he was already dead, they did not break his legs. [34] Instead, one of the soldiers pierced Jesus' side with a spear, bringing a sudden flow of blood and water. [35] The man who saw it has given testimony, and his testimony is true. He knows that he tells the truth, and he testifies so that you also may believe. [36] These things happened so that the scripture would be fulfilled: "Not one of his bones will be broken," [37] and, as another scripture says, "They will look on the one they have pierced."

To be absolutely certain that Jesus had died, one soldier pierced his side with a spear and water and blood came out of the wound. This is because at death the blood and serum (a clear fluid) separate. There can be no question that Jesus was truly dead. He had not fainted only to be resuscitated in the grave later.

Crucifixion was a horrendous method of death. It was a slow, agonizing death that ended finally by suffocation. In Jesus' condition, exhausted and having lost so much blood, he wouldn't have had sufficient oxygen to speak above a whisper. But John tells us that Jesus' last words were a triumphant shout! Even his final act of life was a miracle.

11 Jesus' final words were: "It is finished." Another translation of this would be: "It is accomplished." What had Jesus accomplished for all mankind?

Live what you learn

The late Christian author John Stott puts it brilliantly:

> *"The essence of sin is man substituting himself for God, while the essence of salvation is God substituting himself for man. Man asserts himself against God and puts himself where only God deserves to be; God sacrifices himself for man and puts himself where only man deserves to be."*

The Bible says our central problem is trying to be God and thinking we know best how to run our own lives. The Bible says the solution to our problem is Jesus' death on the cross:

> "He committed no sin, and no deceit was found in his mouth ... He himself bore our sins" in his body on the cross, so that we might die to sins and live for righteousness; "by his wounds you have been healed." (1 Peter 2 v 22, 24).

> God made him who had no sin to be sin for us, so that in him we might become the righteousness of God. (2 Corinthians 5 v 21)

The law of karma says, "You sin, you pay!" But the gospel says, "You sin—and Jesus pays!" Because of God's great love for us, Christ substituted himself for us sinners. We can't earn our way to heaven. We can only accept what Jesus did for us on the cross when he lived the life we were meant to live and faced the judgment we deserved.

What does it mean to you to know that God loves us too much to lose us; that he was willing to move heaven and earth to bring us back into a relationship with him—at whatever the cost to himself—by sending Jesus, his Son?

> *"When a man is getting better he understands more and more clearly that evil is still left in him. When a man is getting worse, he understands his badness less and less. A moderately bad man knows he is not very good: a thoroughly bad man thinks he is all right."*

C. S. LEWIS, *MERE CHRISTIANITY*

Notes

7

The end of doubt

The end of doubt

Question

Imagine yourself as one of Jesus' disciples who has followed him faithfully, and then has just witnessed his crucifixion and burial. What do you feel? What questions would you ask?

Historical context

Those days following the crucifixion were undoubtedly the worst days of the disciples' lives. They must have been filled with despair and unanswered questions. Surely they wondered why Jesus did not escape when the guards came to arrest him in Gethsemane. Why did Jesus deliberately give himself over to them? Why did he insist on dying? None of it made any sense.

When Jesus died, it seemed his cause had suffered permanent defeat. His closest followers were bewildered and grief-stricken. Many had made great sacrifices to follow him. They believed he was the promised Messiah just as he had said he was. He had performed supernatural acts, and healed the blind and sick, and even raised Lazarus from the dead, but now he himself was dead. Two of the Jewish religious leaders, members of the ruling counsil and secret believers in Christ, asked Pilate for Jesus' body and put him in a tomb. Jesus' friends also brought spices for the embalming. Yards of cloth were wrapped around the body with many pounds of spices laid between layers. A very heavy stone (that would have required many men to remove) was rolled in front of the tomb to cover the door. Expert soldiers were ordered to guard the tomb.

Early on the first day of the week, while it was still dark, Mary Magdalene went to the tomb and saw that the stone had been removed from the entrance. ² So she came running to Simon Peter and the other disciple, the one Jesus loved, and said, "They have taken the Lord out of the tomb, and we don't know where they have put him!"

³ So Peter and the other disciple started for the tomb. ⁴ Both were running, but the other disciple outran Peter and reached the tomb first. ⁵ He bent over and looked in at the strips of linen lying there but did not go in. ⁶ Then Simon Peter came along behind him and went straight into the tomb. He saw the strips of linen lying there, ⁷ as well as the cloth that had been wrapped around Jesus' head. The cloth was still lying in its place, separate from the linen. ⁸ Finally the other disciple, who had reached the tomb first, also went inside. He saw and believed. ⁹ (They still did not understand from Scripture that Jesus had to rise from the dead.) ¹⁰ Then the disciples went back to where they were staying.

1. Visualize the scene in verses 1-2. (What did Mary Magdalene see? How do you think she felt? What does she think has happened?)

2. What is the reaction of Peter and John in verses 3-8?

3. How did they know something supernatural had happened concerning Jesus? What was it that they still didn't understand (v 9)?

Now Mary stood outside the tomb crying. As she wept, she bent over to look into the tomb ¹² and saw two angels in white, seated where Jesus' body had been, one at the head and the other at the foot.

¹³ They asked her, "Woman, why are you crying?"

"They have taken my Lord away," she said, "and I don't know where they have put him." ¹⁴ At this, she turned around and saw Jesus standing there, but she did not realize that it was Jesus.

¹⁵ He asked her, "Woman, why are you crying? Who is it you are looking for?"

Thinking he was the gardener, she said, "Sir, if you have carried him away, tell me where you have put him, and I will get him."

¹⁶ Jesus said to her, "Mary."

She turned toward him and cried out in Aramaic, "Rabboni!" (which means "Teacher").

¹⁷ Jesus said, "Do not hold on to me, for I have not yet ascended to the Father. Go instead to my brothers and tell them, 'I am ascending to my Father and your Father, to my God and your God.'"

¹⁸ Mary Magdalene went to the disciples with the news: "I have seen the Lord!" And she told them that he had said these things to her.

4 Describe Mary's state of mind from verses 11-14.

5 After she does recognize Jesus, what stands out to you about their encounter?

6 Why does Jesus tell Mary not to hold on to him (v 17)? What is the significance of Jesus' saying to Mary, "*my* Father and *your* Father" (v 17, italics added)?

READ SOURCE TEXT: JOHN 20 v 19-29

On the evening of that first day of the week, when the disciples were together, with the doors locked for fear of the Jewish leaders, Jesus came and stood among them and said, "Peace be with you!" ²⁰ After he said this, he showed them his hands and side. The disciples were overjoyed when they saw the Lord.

²¹ Again Jesus said, "Peace be with you! As the Father has sent me, I am sending you." ²² And with that he breathed on them and said, "Receive the Holy Spirit. ²³ If you forgive anyone's sins, their

sins are forgiven; if you do not forgive them, they are not forgiven."

²⁴ Now Thomas (also known as Didymus), one of the Twelve, was not with the disciples when Jesus came. ²⁵ So the other disciples told him, "We have seen the Lord!"

But he said to them, "Unless I see the nail marks in his hands and put my finger where the nails were, and put my hand into his side, I will not believe."

²⁶ A week later his disciples were in the house again, and Thomas was with them. Though the doors were locked, Jesus came and stood among them and said, "Peace be with you!" ²⁷ Then he said to Thomas, "Put your finger here; see my hands. Reach out your hand and put it into my side. Stop doubting and believe."

²⁸ Thomas said to him, "My Lord and my God!"

²⁹ Then Jesus told him, "Because you have seen me, you have believed; blessed are those who have not seen and yet have believed."

7 What do you think was the emotional state of the disciples as they hid behind closed doors (v 19)?

We know from Luke's Gospel that the disciples thought they were seeing a ghost!

8 What does Jesus mean when he says twice, "Peace be with you"?

9 Why does Jesus show them his hands and side?

10 Why does Thomas have a problem believing the disciples' story (v 24-25)?

11 Why does Jesus speak to Thomas in the way that he does?

12 What exactly does Thomas come to believe about Jesus (v 28)?

13 We have seen two kinds of doubt in the Gospel of John: first, the doubt of closed unbelief that says, "My mind is made up; don't confuse me with the facts"; second, the doubt that would like to believe but needs more evidence. Which kind of doubt did Thomas have?

Live what you learn

When Jesus revealed his wounds to the disciples, after he rose from the dead, he was saying in effect: *I can give you wholeness, a fresh start and a new beginning because I paid the price for all sin! Put your hand in mine. Believe in me, acknowledge your sin and receive my gift of peace and eternal life which comes from being restored to a right relationship with God.*

When we put our trust in Christ, God meets us in our brokenness, he walks alongside of us in love, and he asks us to show others the same grace we have received from God.

John 20 v 31 goes on to say:

> These [things] are written that you may believe that Jesus is the Messiah, the Son of God, and that by believing you may have life in his name.

What, if anything, stops you from believing that Jesus is the Messiah and the Son of God? Or, if you *do* believe this, what are the implications for you?

"When I go down to the grave, I can say like so many others that I have finished my day's work; but I cannot say that I have finished my life. Another day's work will begin the next morning. The tomb is not a blind alley—it is a thoroughfare. It closes with the twilight to open with the dawn."

VICTOR HUGO

Victor Hugo (1802-1885) was a French nineteenth-century novelist, poet, playwright and leader of the Romantic movement. Hugo's two best-known novels are *The Hunchback of Notre Dame* and *Les Misérables*. Hugo was celebrated as a great humanitarian, but the death of his daughter, Leopoldine, in his mid-life caused a profound spiritual crisis that led him to explore spiritual issues. His "Last Will and Testament" contains the clearest declaration of his religious beliefs. In his will, Hugo doesn't describe himself in othodox Christian terms but more as a Christian mystic. Yet few writers have captured the Christian understanding of grace more powerfully than Hugo's character Jean Valjean in *Les Misérables*.

Notes

More from Becky Pippert MINISTRIES

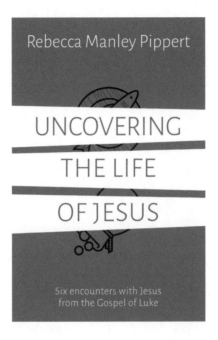

Rebecca Manley Pippert

UNCOVERING THE LIFE OF JESUS

Six encounters with Jesus
from the Gospel of Luke

Meet a woman with a bad reputation crashing a party; a runaway son who's squandered his inheritance; a beggar at the roadside who won't shut up; a man who's incredibly rich but intensely hated. And at the center of it all, meet Jesus.

Uncover the life of Jesus in six studies from Luke's Gospel.

"Excellent and highly recommended."

Richard, Customer website review

thegoodbook.com | thegoodbook.co.uk | thegoodbook.com.au

thegood**book**
COMPANY

More from *Becky Pippert* MINISTRIES

Christianity offers newness—new life, new future, new perspectives, new priorities. But what does this look like for you? Join Becky Manley Pippert as she helps us see how we can, and why we should, live as followers of Jesus.

The three parts of this course will help you get going, keep growing and go deeper in your Christian journey.

"Clear and accessible, yet substantial and thoughtful explorations of how to be grounded and grow in Christian faith."

Tim Keller, Founding Pastor of Redeemer Presbyterian Church, New York

thegoodbook.com | thegoodbook.co.uk | thegoodbook.com.au

thegoodbook
COMPANY

Thanks for reading this book. We hope you enjoyed it, and found it helpful.

Most people want to find answers to the big questions of life: Who are we? Why are we here? How should we live? But for many valid reasons we are often unable to find the time or the right space to think positively and carefully about them.

Perhaps you have questions that you need an answer for. Perhaps you have met Christians who have seemed unsympathetic or incomprehensible. Or maybe you are someone who has grown up believing, but need help to make things a little clearer.

At The Good Book Company, we're passionate about producing materials that help people of all ages and stages understand the heart of the Christian message, which is found in the pages of the Bible.

Whoever you are, and wherever you are at when it comes to these big questions, we hope we can help. As a publisher we want to help you look at the good book that is the Bible because we're convinced that as we meet the person who stands at its centre—Jesus Christ—we find the clearest answers to our biggest questions.

Visit our website to discover the range of books, videos and other resources we produce, or visit our partner site www.christianityexplored.org for a clear explanation of who Jesus is and why he came.

Thanks again for reading,

Your friends at The Good Book Company

thegoodbook.com | thegoodbook.co.uk
thegoodbook.com.au | thegoodbook.co.nz

WWW.CHRISTIANITYEXPLORED.ORG

Our partner site is a great place to explore the Christian faith, with powerful testimonies and answers to difficult questions.